KINGSTO... W9-BCD-247

3 2386 00159 2901

J
292.13   Shone, Rob.
Sho   Greek myths.

New
10/26/09   New 10/26/09

$29.25   1592901

DATE			

DISCARDED

Duplicate

KINGSTON LIBRARY
55 FRANKLIN STREET
KINGSTON, NY 12401
(845) 331-0507

BAKER & TAYLOR

GRAPHIC MYTHOLOGY

GREEK MYTHS

by Rob Shone

KINGSTON LIBRARY
55 Franklin Street
Kingston, NY 12401

rosen
central™

The Rosen Publishing Group, Inc., New York

Published in 2006 by The Rosen Publishing Group, Inc.
29 East 21st Street, New York, NY 10010

Copyright © 2006 David West Books

First edition, 2006

All rights reserved. No part of this book may be reproduced in any form without permission in writing from the publisher, except by a reviewer.

Designed and produced by
David West Books

Editor: Kate Newport

Photo credits:
    Page 4 top, Andy Didya/iStockphoto.com

Library of Congress Cataloging-in-Publication Data

Shone, Rob.
  Greek myths / by Rob Shone.
      p. cm. – (Graphic mythology)
  Includes index.
  ISBN 1-4042-0801-1 (library binding) – ISBN 1-4042-0813-5 (pbk.)
  ISBN 1-4042-6253-9 (6 pack)
  1. Mythology, Greek–Juvenile literature. I. Title. II. Series.
  BL782.S53 2005
  292.1'3–dc22

                                    2005019283

Manufactured in China

CONTENTS

KINGSTON LIBRARY
55 FRANKLIN STREET
KINGSTON, NY 12401
(845) 331-0507

J
292.13
Sho

159 2901

THE GREEK WORLD

The ancient Greeks were a very superstitious people and they worshipped many gods and goddesses. They did not have all the scientific knowledge we have today, so the Greeks relied on stories or myths about their gods to explain the world around them.

TEMPLES AND WORSHIP

The Greeks built many temples dedicated to particular gods. Priests and priestesses lived at these temples and performed special services or rituals each day. Ancient Greeks would pray at the temples and leave presents, such as olive oil, wine, and animals to encourage the gods to hear their prayers. The ancient Greeks also believed they had to ask the gods about any important events or decisions in their lives.

ORACLES AND WORSHIP

Sometimes the Greeks would visit a special priest or priestess, called an oracle, in order to learn what would happen in the future. The oracle would go into a trance to find out, and then their answers would be translated by a priest. One very famous oracle was at Delphi. Here a priestess called the Pythia would consult the god Apollo.

Perseus was a great Greek hero. He is famous for killing the Gorgon Medusa.

MYTHS AND LEGEND

Why did the Greeks tell stories? Some stories came from the need to find meaning in everyday life. Other tales were meant to make the listener think about the faults of humans. Others were invented simply to delight and entertain. The earliest Greeks told myths about the gods, but as time went on, legends developed that also described the adventures of famous heroes. For example, the legend of Jason was based on a real journey that we think took place around 1400 B.C. However, by the time it was first written down about 1,000 years later, it had become a supernatural tale involving the gods and terrible monsters. We can see from this how oral storytelling has given us the Greek myths we know today.

This is the Acropolis in Athens. It was built in the fifth century B.C. and contained many sacred shrines.

Hercules was one of the most popular heroes in ancient Greece. He is shown here defeating the dragon Ladon.

THREE GREEK MYTHS

These tales, about three different adventurers, are typical Greek stories that explore basic themes about human nature, bravery, and being smarter than your enemies.

Jason
The son of the lawful king of Iolcus. His uncle Pelias had usurped the throne.

JASON AND THE ARGONAUTS

Jason is the famous hero who uses his bravery and quick thinking to find the Golden Fleece and win back the throne from his evil uncle Pelias. In order to do this, he must find a heroic crew for his ship the *Argo*, fight terrible creatures such as the dragon's tooth army and the harpies, and find out how to survive the Clashing Rocks. Along the way he is helped by the goddess Hera, who wants to destroy Pelias, and Medea, who falls in love with him.

Medea
The daughter of Aeetes, the king of Colchis. A powerful sorceress and priestess of Hecate.

The Golden Fleece
The fleece (coat) of a ram that had once saved the boy Phrixus from sacrifice by carrying him through the air to Colchis. Aeetes then helped the boy and placed the fleece in a sacred grove guarded by a dragon.

Pelias
King of Iolcus, and Jason's uncle. He stole the throne from Jason's father.

ICARUS

The story of Icarus is still told today to warn people against carelessness, greed, and disobedience. Daedalus builds two sets of wings so that he and his son can escape from their prison on Crete. However, these will only work if they do not fly too close to the sun.

Daedalus and Icarus
Daedalus was a great Athenian inventor who built the famous labyrinth for King Minos of Crete. After this, Minos kept Daedalus and his son Icarus prisoner.

Hercules

The son of Zeus and a mortal woman. His name is more commonly spelled Heracles. Hera, the wife of Zeus, was jealous of Hercules as he was the product of an affair. Zeus tried to make up for this by naming the child after Hera, hence Heracles.

Eurystheus

Hercules' cousin and king of Mycenae. Hera had tricked her husband Zeus into making him king instead of Hercules.

Iolaus

Hercules' friend and faithful servant who helped him defeat the fearful Hydra.

THE LABORS OF HERCULES

The Greeks loved stories of heroic deeds, and Hercules was perhaps the greatest hero of all. As a young man, Hercules had already proven himself an expert with a bow and arrow, a champion wrestler, and the possessor of superhuman strength. Eventually, out of jealousy, Hera drove Hercules mad, and in a frenzy he killed his own wife and children. As a punishment for his crimes, he was sentenced to perform a set of tasks, also known as labors. The labors were set by his cousin King Eurystheus.

JASON AND THE ARGONAUTS

THE GODDESS HERA WANTED REVENGE. PELIAS, KING OF IOLCUS, HAD ANGERED HER BY MURDERING HIS STEPMOTHER, SIDERO, AT THE ALTAR OF HERA'S TEMPLE. HERA HAD BEEN PATIENT. NOW SHE SAW HER CHANCE. ONE DAY, OUTSIDE THE ROYAL PALACE...

I AM JASON. I WISH TO SEE MY UNCLE, KING PELIAS.

JASON?! I THOUGHT MY NEPHEW HAD DIED AS A BABY, ALONG WITH HIS MOTHER! HMM, HE COULD MAKE TROUBLE FOR ME!

JASON! WELCOME HOME! WHERE HAVE YOU BEEN ALL THESE YEARS?

UNCLE...?

...WITH CHEIRON, THE CENTAUR. HE HAS BEEN MY TEACHER SINCE I WAS A BABY. I HAVE RETURNED TOO LATE, THOUGH. MY FATHER ... HE IS DEAD.

YES, JASON. WE ALL MISS HIM.

I BECAME THE COUNTRY'S RULER AFTER YOUR FATHER DIED.

BUT UNCLE, SINCE MY FATHER WAS THE OLDER BROTHER, SHOULDN'T I NOW BE KING?

CHEIRON MADE JASON'S TASK KNOWN THROUGHOUT GREECE. MANY HEROES, READY FOR AN ADVENTURE, CAME TO IOLCUS. AMONG THEM WERE ORPHEUS, TELAMON, CASTOR, AND POLLUX. EVEN HERCULES, THE GREATEST HERO OF ALL, JOINED THEM FOR A SHORT TIME.

MEANWHILE...

HERE SHE IS, JASON. LEAN, FAST, AND SHALLOW-HULLED.

SHE'S BEAUTIFUL, ARGO.

JASON NAMED THE SHIP ARGO, AFTER ITS BUILDER. ITS CREW OF HEROES WERE CALLED THE ARGONAUTS. FINALLY, THEY SET OFF ON THEIR QUEST.

ON THE WAY, THEY STOPPED AT AN ISLAND TO COLLECT SUPPLIES.

SUDDENLY...

LOOK OUT!

WHAT ARE THEY?

THEY'RE THE GEGENEES!

HERCULES, WHO HAD STAYED BEHIND, HELD OFF THE SIX-ARMED MONSTERS UNTIL THE REST OF THE CREW RETURNED.

THEY SAILED ON TO THRACE.

WELCOME STRANGERS! I AM THE SEER, PHINEUS.

ZEUS TOOK AWAY MY SIGHT FOR TELLING TOO MANY OF HIS SECRETS. I KNOW THAT YOU ARE GOING TO COLCHIS AND I CAN HELP YOU GET THERE, BUT FIRST YOU MUST HELP ME.

JASON DID WHAT PHINEUS TOLD HIM...

WAIT UNTIL THE DOVE HAS PASSED BETWEEN THE ROCKS.

THE ROCKS CLOSED IN ON THE BIRD, CLASHED AND STARTED TO OPEN.

NOW! IF YOU WANT TO SEE GREECE AGAIN, BEND YOUR BACKS, AND ROW!

THE ARGO RACED THROUGH THE GAP BEFORE THE ROCKS COULD CLOSE AGAIN.

THE ARGONAUTS SAILED ON.

SOON, THE ARGO REACHED AEA, THE CAPITAL OF COLCHIS.

AT THE HARBOR...

WELCOME, STRANGERS. I AM MEDEA, DAUGHTER OF KING AEETES.

MEANWHILE, HERA'S PLANS WERE BEGINNING TO TAKE SHAPE. SHE CAUSED MEDEA TO FALL IN LOVE WITH JASON.

A FEAST WAS HELD IN THEIR HONOR.

NORMALLY, WE DON'T LIKE STRANGERS, JASON. BUT YOU ARE MY DAUGHTER'S GUEST, SO YOU ARE ALSO MINE.

JASON TOLD KING AEETES WHY HE NEEDED THE FLEECE.

THE FLEECE IS SACRED TO US. BUT IT WOULD BE IMPOLITE TO REFUSE A GUEST.

I SHALL GIVE IT TO YOU, JASON, BUT THERE IS SOMETHING YOU MUST DO FOR ME IN RETURN...

HE YOKED THE BULLS TOGETHER AND SOWED THE DRAGON'S TEETH.

JASON REMEMBERED MEDEA'S WORDS. HE PICKED UP A STONE AND...

DINNNG

THE DRAGON TOOTH SOLDIER THOUGHT HIS NEIGHBOR HAD HIT HIM AND STRUCK OUT. SOON, THEY WERE ALL FIGHTING EACH OTHER...

...UNTIL NOT ONE WAS LEFT ALIVE.

MY FATHER WILL NOT LET YOU LEAVE WITH THE FLEECE, JASON. WE MUST TAKE IT TONIGHT!

LATER...

LOOK, THE FLEECE HANGS ON THAT TREE. BUT IT IS GUARDED!

SPRINKLE THIS POTION OVER THE DRAGON. IT WILL MAKE IT SLEEP.

AS THE DRAGON SLEPT...

THE ARGONAUTS FACED MANY DANGERS ON THEIR RETURN JOURNEY. ON THE ISLAND OF CRETE...

IT IS TALUS! THE LAST OF THE BRONZE MEN!

ONCE AGAIN, MEDEA'S MAGIC SAVED THEM. SHE CAUSED A ROCK TO SLIP FROM THE GIANT'S HANDS...

...AND ONTO HIS ONE WEAK SPOT.

JASON FINALLY REACHES IOLCUS.

PELIAS! HERE IS YOUR FLEECE. NOW GIVE ME THE THRONE!

JASON! HOW?

JASON! YOU HAVE **THE FLEECE!** YOU MUST BE TIRED. REST FIRST, YOU SHALL SOON HAVE THE CROWN.

I NEED TIME TO GET RID OF HIM!

KING PELIAS IS ASLEEP. YOU **MUST** DO THIS FOR THE MAGIC TO WORK. TAKE YOUR DAGGERS AND STRIKE HIM HARD, THEN POUR THE POTION OVER HIM. SOON HE WILL BECOME YOUNG AGAIN, AND YOU SHALL SEE THE FATHER YOU KNEW AS CHILDREN.

QUICKLY SISTER, THE POTION!

WHY IS NOTHING HAPPENING?!

FATHER!

THE POTION WAS FAKE.

WE HAVE KILLED HIM!!

PELIAS WAS DEAD, HERA GOT HER REVENGE FOR SIDERO'S MURDER, AND JASON HAD BECOME KING OF IOLCUS. THE QUEST FOR THE FLEECE WAS JASON'S LAST GREAT ADVENTURE.

THE END

HOME! ATHENS! MINOS IS A CRUEL TYRANT. HE KEEPS ME HERE BECAUSE I HELPED MY FELLOW ATHENIANS.

THEY WERE TO BE FED TO THAT HALF-MAN, HALF-BULL, SON OF HIS...THE MINOTAUR! I HAD TO HELP THEM.

FATHER, I'VE GOT YOU SOME FEATH...*GASP!*

MINOS MAY RULE THIS ISLAND, AND ITS SEAS, BUT HE DOES NOT RULE THE SKIES!

I DIDN'T LIE, ICARUS. SOON, WE WILL ESCAPE FROM THIS ISLAND AND GO HOME.

THESE FEATHERS YOU HAVE BROUGHT ARE THE LAST FEW I NEED TO FINISH OUR WINGS. THEY WILL BE READY TOMORROW!

FATHER AND SON FLY FROM THEIR PRISON.

EVENTUALLY THEY REACH THE SEA...THEY ARE FREE.

THE FARTHER THEY FLY, THE MORE ICARUS ENJOYS HIS NEW SKILL. SOON, HE FORGETS HIS FATHER'S WARNING.

HE FLIES HIGHER...

...AND HIGHER UNTIL...

...THE WAX HOLDING THE FEATHERS IN PLACE MELTS IN THE HOT SUN.

THE LABORS OF HERCULES

HERCULES HAD FOLLOWED THE GREAT LION FOR MONTHS...

...AT LAST, THE BEAST WAS CORNERED.

ONE FINAL DASH AND...

HERCULES' CLUB AND ARROWS HAD BEEN USELESS AGAINST THE LION'S THICK MANE. HE WOULD HAVE TO KILL IT WITH HIS BARE HANDS!

THE TERROR OF THE NEMEA VALLEY WAS DEAD – STRANGLED. HERCULES HAD COMPLETED HIS FIRST TASK.

WHY HAD HERCULES KILLED THE LION? IN A FIT OF MADNESS BROUGHT ON BY HIS STEPMOTHER, THE GODDESS HERA, HERCULES HAD KILLED HIS OWN WIFE AND CHILDREN. TO PUNISH HIM, THE GODS HAD FORCED HERCULES TO SERVE HIS COUSIN, EURYSTHEUS, THE KING OF MYCENAE, AND PERFORM TEN HEROIC TASKS, OR LABORS. HERCULES WAS NOW BACK IN MYCENAE TO BE GIVEN HIS SECOND TASK.

AT THE COURT OF KING EURYSTHEUS...

WAKE UP, SIRE.

WHAA?

ARGH! THE NEMEAN LION HAS COME TO EAT ME!

...HERE IS ITS SKIN.

THE NEMEAN LION IS DEAD...

ER, WELL DONE, HERCULES. YOU KEEP IT. SOMEONE WILL GIVE YOU YOUR NEXT TASK. I HAVE TO GO.

THE MAN'S A MENACE! IN THE FUTURE, DON'T LET HIM NEAR THE PALACE! WHO KNOWS WHAT DAMAGE HE COULD DO?

I NEVER LIKED HIM WHEN WE WERE CHILDREN! WHY COULDN'T HERCULES AND THE LION HAVE KILLED EACH OTHER!

HERCULES, YOU MUST GO TO THE SWAMPS OF ARGOS. THERE, YOU MUST FIND AND KILL THE HYDRA!

BACK IN MYCENAE...

WHERE'S EURYSTHEUS?

HE'S OVER THERE.

AFTER YOUR LAST VISIT EURYSTHEUS HAD THAT LARGE BRONZE POT MADE AND BURIED. HE SAYS HE FEELS SAFER IN IT WHEN YOU'RE AROUND, HERCULES.

GET ON WITH IT!

HERE IS THE THIRD TASK HERCULES...

EURYSTHEUS WANTED THE HIND OF CERYNEIA. THE DEER HAD GOLDEN HORNS AND BRONZE HOOVES AND WAS THE GODDESS DIANA'S PET. HERCULES CHASED THE DEER FOR A YEAR UNTIL HE FINALLY MANAGED TO WOUND AND CATCH IT.

BUT HE WAS STOPPED BY DIANA. WHEN SHE SAW HER WOUNDED PET, SHE BECAME ANGRY. HERCULES EXPLAINED ABOUT THE TASKS AND DIANA FORGAVE HIM. SHE HEALED THE DEER'S WOUND AND LET HERCULES TAKE HER PET TO MYCENAE.

FOR THE NEXT TASK, HERCULES HAD TO GO TO MOUNT ERYMANTHUS. A GIANT BOAR THERE HAD BEEN TERRORIZING THE COUNTRYSIDE. HERCULES HAD TO BRING IT BACK TO MYCENAE – ALIVE!

ON THE WAY TO MYCENAE...

SQUEEEEEEEAL!

WILL YOU JUST STOP YOUR WRIGGLING!

32

FOR THE SIXTH TASK, HERCULES HAD TO DRIVE AWAY A HUGE FLOCK OF BIRDS FROM THE TOWN OF STYMPHALOS.

TO HELP HIM, THE GODDESS ATHENA HAD GIVEN HERCULES A PAIR OF MAGIC CYMBALS.

WHEN THE CYMBALS WERE STRUCK...

KERRANNGGG!!

...THE NOISE SCARED THE BIRDS INTO THE AIR.

THE SIXTH TASK WAS DONE.

HERCULES EASILY CAUGHT THE CRETAN BULL TO COMPLETE THE SEVENTH TASK...

...AND TOOK THE FLESH-EATING HORSES OF DIOMEDES BACK TO EURYSTHEUS FOR THE EIGHTH TASK.

FOR THE NINTH TASK, HERCULES HAD TO BRING BACK THE GIRDLE OF HIPPOLYTA, QUEEN OF THE AMAZONS. ALL WENT WELL. HIPPOLYTA GAVE HER GIRDLE TO HERCULES. AS HERCULES AND HIPPOLYTA WERE SAYING GOOD-BYE, HERA, DISGUISED AS AN AMAZON, SPREAD RUMORS THAT THEIR QUEEN WAS BEING KIDNAPPED. THE AMAZONS ATTACKED HERCULES, AND HIPPOLYTA WAS KILLED.

IN MYCENAE...

I THOUGHT IT WOULD BE FUN HAVING HERCULES AS A SLAVE FOR A WHILE. BUT HE'S CAUSED ME NOTHING BUT TROUBLE!

THE COUNTRYSIDE IS NOW FULL OF ALL THE DANGEROUS BEASTS HE'S BROUGHT BACK.

AND THE PEOPLE THINK HE'S A HERO. WHERE IS HERCULES NOW?

BRINGING YOU THE RED CATTLE OF GERYON, SIRE.

LET'S HOPE HE TAKES HIS TIME.

LADIES AND GENTLEMEN! LOOK! ALL THE TASKS OF HERCULES DECORATE THESE POTS AND VASES...

THE THREE GOLDEN APPLES BELONGED TO HERA AND WERE KEPT IN THE GARDEN OF THE HESPERIDES. THEY WERE GUARDED BY A DRAGON, AND THREE MAIDENS CALLED THE HESPERIDES.

HERCULES DID NOT KNOW WHERE THE GARDEN WAS, OR HOW TO GET THE APPLES, BUT EURYSTHEUS WANTED THEM. HERCULES WENT TO SEE ATLAS, THE HESPERIDES' FATHER...

ATLAS WAS A TITAN, ONE OF THE FIRST GODS. FOR MAKING WAR AGAINST ZEUS, HE HAD BEEN CONDEMNED TO HOLD UP THE HEAVENS FOREVER.

HERCULES EXPLAINED TO ATLAS WHY HE WAS THERE.

AS THEIR FATHER, ONLY YOU CAN PERSUADE THE HESPERIDES TO LEND ME THE GOLDEN APPLES, ATLAS.

HOW CAN I GET THE APPLES, HERCULES? WHAT WOULD HAPPEN TO THE HEAVENS IF I LEFT?

LET ME HOLD THE SKY WHILE YOU ARE GONE.

ONCE IN THE DAYLIGHT...

...CERBERUS WAS BEATEN.

HERCULES TOOK CERBERUS BACK TO MYCENAE.

I WONDER WHAT EURYSTHEUS WILL SAY WHEN HE SEES YOU!

HERE BOY, FETCH!

ONCE EURYSTHEUS HAD SEEN HIM, HERCULES LET CERBERUS RETURN TO HADES. THE LAST TASK HAD BEEN COMPLETED. HERCULES HAD PAID FOR THE MURDER OF HIS FAMILY. HE HAD WON THE RIGHT TO LIVE WITH THE GODS AFTER HIS DEATH. ...AND AS FOR EURYSTHEUS...

...ARE YOU **SURE** THEY'VE GONE?

THE END

MORE MYTHICAL CHARACTERS

Originating from many different myths and legends, Greek mythology is a treasure chest of colorful, larger-than-life characters. Here is a small sample of heroes, kings, monsters, and gods.

ACHILLES — A Greek hero who fought at Troy. Achilles was impossible to harm except for his heel. He killed Hector but was killed by Paris.

APHRODITE — The goddess of love and beauty. She was born fully formed from the sea foam at Paphos in Cyprus.

APOLLO — The god of music and poetry. He was the son of Zeus and was associated with the sun. He was the twin brother of Artemis.

ARES — The son of Zeus and Hera and the god of war.

ARTEMIS — The goddess of the moon and Apollo's twin sister.

ATHENA — The goddess of war and wisdom. She was born, fully formed, from the head of Zeus. Athens was named in her honor.

CENTAURS — A race of creatures that had the body of a human but the legs of a horse. Jason was brought up by Cheiron, a centaur.

HADES — The god of the dead and the brother of Zeus and Poseidon. He kidnapped and married Persephone.

HERA — The wife of Zeus and the goddess of women and marriage. She was the protector of Jason, but the enemy of Hercules and the Trojans.

MEDUSA — The name of the most terrible Gorgon sister. She was mortal, but it was nearly impossible to kill her because one look at her would turn anyone to stone. Perseus used mirrors to fight and kill her. When she died, Pegasus sprang from her spilt blood.

MINOTAUR — A creature that was half man and half bull. He was the son of Pasophae (wife of Minos) and a bull from the sea. Minos kept him in the labyrinth made by Daedalus, and fed him on Athenian youths. He was eventually killed by Theseus with Ariadne's help.

PANDORA — The first woman. Pandora was made by Hephaestus and became the wife of Epimetheus. Zeus gave her a box, which she was told not to open. After a while, her curiosity took over and she opened it. All the evils of the world flew out of the box and only hope was left in the bottom.

PEGASUS — A winged horse that sprang from the blood of Medusa, after she was killed by Perseus. Pegasus later became a constellation and was the servant of Zeus.

PERSEUS — The son of Zeus and Danae, he and his mother were put in a chest and thrown into the sea by Acrisius, Danae's father. Perseus grew up to defeat Medusa the Gorgon. He then used her head to rescue Andromeda.

POSEIDON — The god of water and the sea. Poseidon was the brother of Zeus and Hades and is usually shown with a trident in his hand.

THESEUS — The king and national hero of Athens, Theseus is most famous for conquering the Amazons and killing the Minotaur.

THE TITANS — The twelve children of Uranus and Gaea. They were the older generation of gods. Zeus and Hera were the children of Cronus, one of the Titans. When Zeus and the Olympians took power, the Titans made war on them and the Titans were defeated.

ZEUS — The god of the sky and the supreme Olympian, Zeus was married to Hera, and was also the father of Hercules and Perseus.

GLOSSARY

Amazon A member of a nation of women warriors from Scythia.

Athenian A person who lives in or comes from Athens in Greece.

betrayed To have turned against someone.

capital The main city in a country and the seat of its government.

condemned To be blamed or punished for a crime.

conquer To defeat another land using weapons.

constellation A group of stars.

girdle A belt that goes around the wearer's waist.

grove A small group of trees.

harpies Vicious winged monsters with the head and body of a woman, and the tail, wings, and claws of a bird.

hind A female deer.

Hydra A giant snake with many heads.

inventor Somebody who first designs or makes an item.

labors Tasks such as those performed by Hercules.

labyrinth A structure with many passages that is hard to get out of.

maiden A young woman.

ointment A sticky liquid that is applied to heal or protect someone.

oracle Someone who is considered to be very wise and can predict the future. An oracle can also talk with the gods.

potion A magic liquid that is either medicinal or poisonous.

prophecy A prediction of the future.

revenge To get even with someone who has hurt you by doing something unpleasant to him or her.

sacred When something is religious or holy.

seer A prophet who sees visions of the future.

sow To plant seeds in the ground.

superstitious A fear of the unknown or of religion or magic.

terrorize To fill someone with fear or dread.

trident A spear or scepter with three prongs like a fork.

tyrant A king or leader who rules through fear and cruelty.

underworld The world of the dead, which is underneath the world of the living.

usurp To take control of a throne or position illegally.

worship Ceremonies and prayers dedicated to a god or gods.

yoke A wooden bar used to attach a plow to cows or oxen.

FOR MORE INFORMATION

ORGANIZATIONS

Fine Arts Museums of San Francisco
Legion of Honor
34th Avenue & Clement Street
Lincoln Park
San Francisco, CA 94121
(415) 750-3600
Web site: http://www.thinker.org/legion

J. Paul Getty Museum
1200 Getty Center Drive
Los Angeles, CA 90049-1687
(310) 440-7330
Web site: http://www.getty.edu/museum

The Metropolitan Museum of Art
1000 Fifth Avenue
New York, NY 10028-0198
(212) 535-7710
Web site: http://www.metmuseum.org

FOR FURTHER READING

Bellingham, David. *The Kingfisher Book of Mythology: Gods, Goddesses and Heroes from Around the World*. London, England: Kingfisher Publications Plc., 2001.

Burrell, Roy. *First Ancient History*. New York, NY: Oxford University Press, Inc., 1999.

Philip, Neil. *The Illustrated Book of Myth*. London, England: Dorling Kindersley, 1995.

INDEX

Web Sites

Due to the changing nature of Internet links, the Rosen Publishing Group, Inc., has developed an online list of Web sites related to the subject of this book. This site is updated regularly. Please use this link to access the list:
http://www.rosenlinks.com/gm/greek